God Made You, My Darling Boy

"This book is an affirmation of who our boys were made to be: godly men who are strong, wise, and loving. I picture my own son as I read these words!"

—Phylicia Masonheimer
Author of *Every Woman a Theologian*

"I can't imagine a better motivation for writing a children's book than Kelsie's expressed purpose in writing this one: she went looking for a book to read to her young son about the unique, God-given wonders of being a boy and couldn't find one. As a parent and grandparent of boys, I am thrilled that Kelsie has written this delightful book to affirm God's unchanging truth and encourage little boys to fully embrace who He created them to be. It's so refreshing to see a young mom shine a light in the midst of so much cultural confusion about gender issues."

—Mary Ann Crum
Newspaper columnist, Podcaster of *Unquenchable Hope*,
Author of *A Giggle Goes a Long Way* and *Live. Learn. LAUGH!*

"As someone who has suffered a public attack for standing up for the fact that boys are boys and girls are girls, I can tell you that it is a very brave thing that Kelsie has done to write this book and a brave thing that her publisher is doing to publish it. I hope the day comes when the statement I just made sounds odd to the reader. But until then, thank you for this 'must-read' for parents, teachers, and family ministry leaders in need of a sensitive, well-written narrative for children on the subject of gender identity."

—Angela J. Didway, M.S., LPC
Licensed Professional Counselor, specializing in children & families
Owner, Maximum Child Learning Center
Founder & CEO, Maximum Elementary Christian School

"Now is the time, Mom and Dad, to teach your young son how very special he is to be created by God as a boy. Kelsie Detweiler does a beautiful job intertwining God's Word in *God Made You, My Darling Boy* in a way that will lovingly open up your son's eyes to God's truth. Unfortunately, the world is teaching our children otherwise! This invaluable, illustrated book will be a joy to read aloud to your little one over and over again."

—Kirby King
Speaker and author of *Abiding in Christ—What is it Anyway?*
and *Walking Through Fire Without Getting Burned*

(continued on last page)

God Made You, My Darling Boy

BY
KELSIE DETWEILER

Ambassador International
Greenville, South Carolina & Belfast, Northern Ireland
www.ambassador-international.com

God Made You, My Darling Boy

©2024 by By Kelsie Detweiler

All rights reserved

Hardcover ISBN: 978-1-64960-424-8

Paperback ISBN: 978-1-64960-647-1

eISBN: 978-1-64960-472-9

Edited by Katie Cruice Smith

Illustrated by Garin Adi S

Interior Typesetting by Karen Slayne

Scripture used is from the Holy Bible, New International Version®, NIV® Copyright ©1973, 1978, 1984, 2011 by Biblica, Inc.® Used by permission. All rights reserved worldwide.

AMBASSADOR INTERNATIONAL

Emerald House

411 University Ridge, Suite B14

Greenville, SC 29601, USA

www.ambassador-international.com

AMBASSADOR BOOKS

The Mount

2 Woodstock Link

Belfast, BT6 8DD, Northern Ireland, UK

www.ambassadormedia.co.uk

The colophon is a trademark of Ambassador, a Christian publishing company.

For Elias, my darling boy.

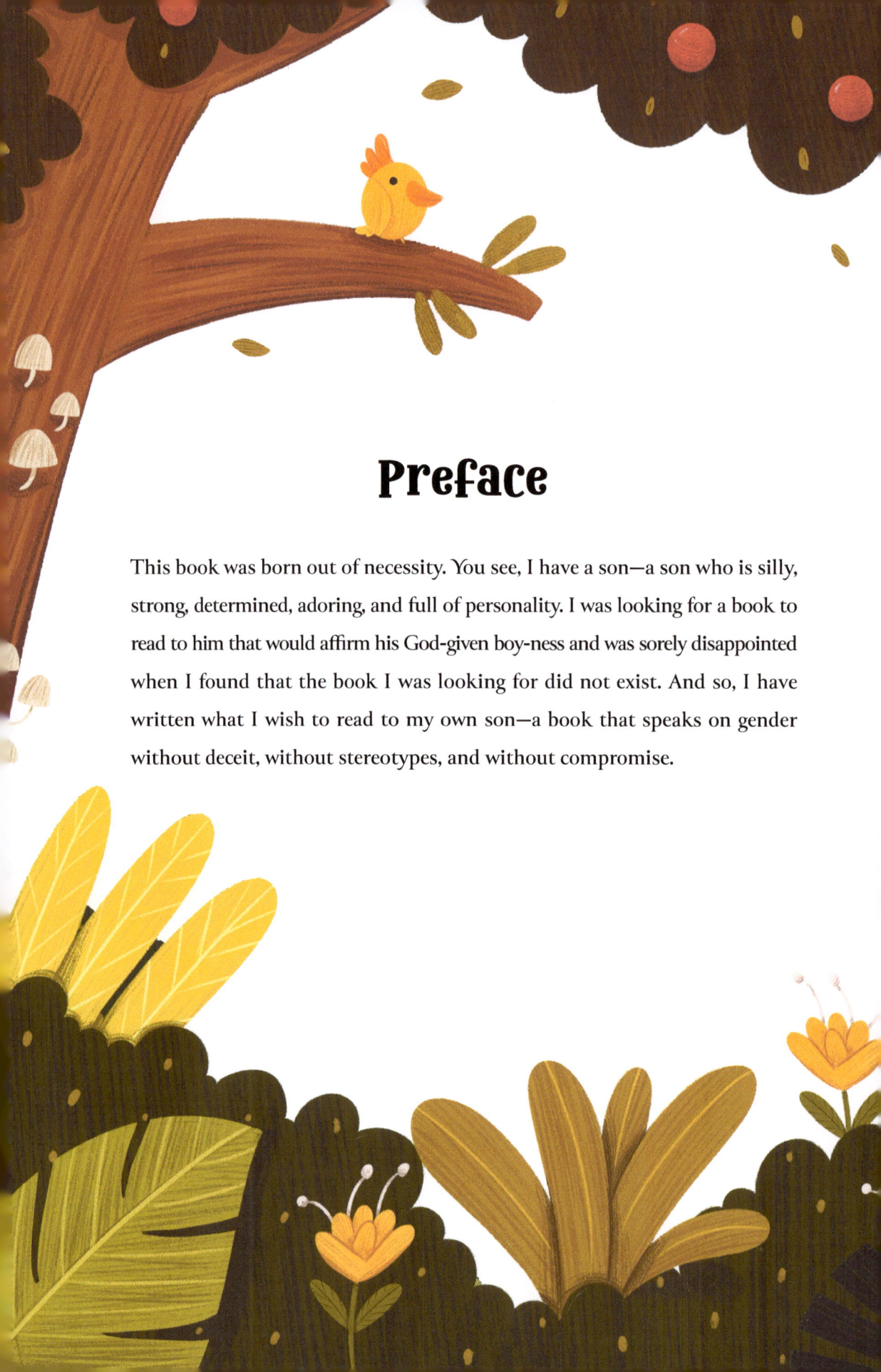

Preface

This book was born out of necessity. You see, I have a son—a son who is silly, strong, determined, adoring, and full of personality. I was looking for a book to read to him that would affirm his God-given boy-ness and was sorely disappointed when I found that the book I was looking for did not exist. And so, I have written what I wish to read to my own son—a book that speaks on gender without deceit, without stereotypes, and without compromise.

A Note to Parents

In today's culture, children are exposed to an alarming amount of gender ideology that is contrary to God's Word. In Genesis 1:27, we are told, "In the image of God he created him; male and female he created them." Now, more than ever, we need to be speaking and reading to our children in ways that truthfully affirm their God-given gender. Not only is their boy-ness or girl-ness something that makes them unique, but it is a gift from God and, furthermore, a gift to the rest of humanity.

It is, indeed, God Who determines one's gender, and His designs are never an accident. Psalm 139:13-16 reminds us that our inward parts were formed by God, that no part of us was hidden from God, and that every single day appointed to us was written in His book even before they came to be. What a comfort! I hope this book and its companion, *God Made You, My Darling Girl,* will serve as a tool in your hands as you train your children in the way they should go and that you will daily encourage your children that they were created with a purposeful design by a loving God.

For you formed my inward parts; you knitted me together in my mother's womb. I praise you, for I am fearfully and wonderfully made. Wonderful are your works; my soul knows it very well. My frame was not hidden from you when I was being made in secret, intricately woven in the depths of the earth. Your eyes saw my unformed substance; in your book were written, every one of them, the days that were formed for me, when as yet there was none of them.

—Psalm 139:13-16

When a baby is born and
the doctor says,

"it's a boy"

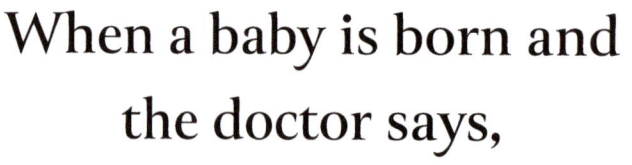

everyone shares a smile.
Why are they so happy?

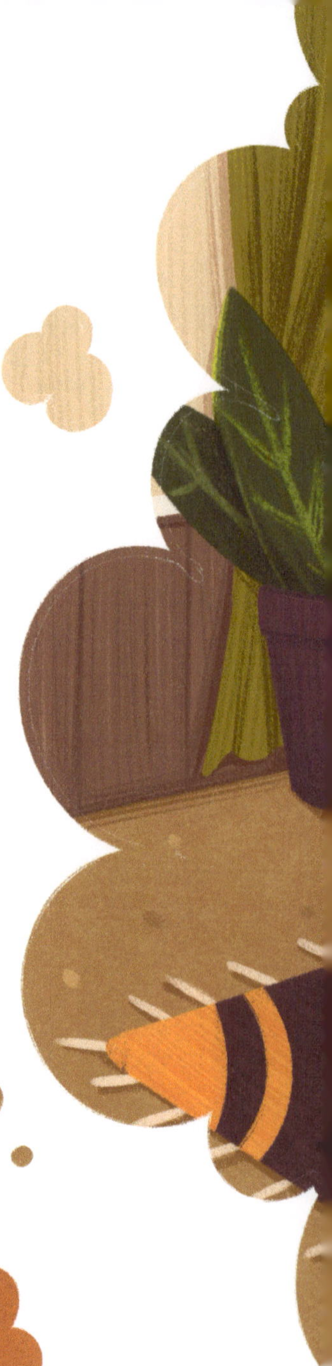

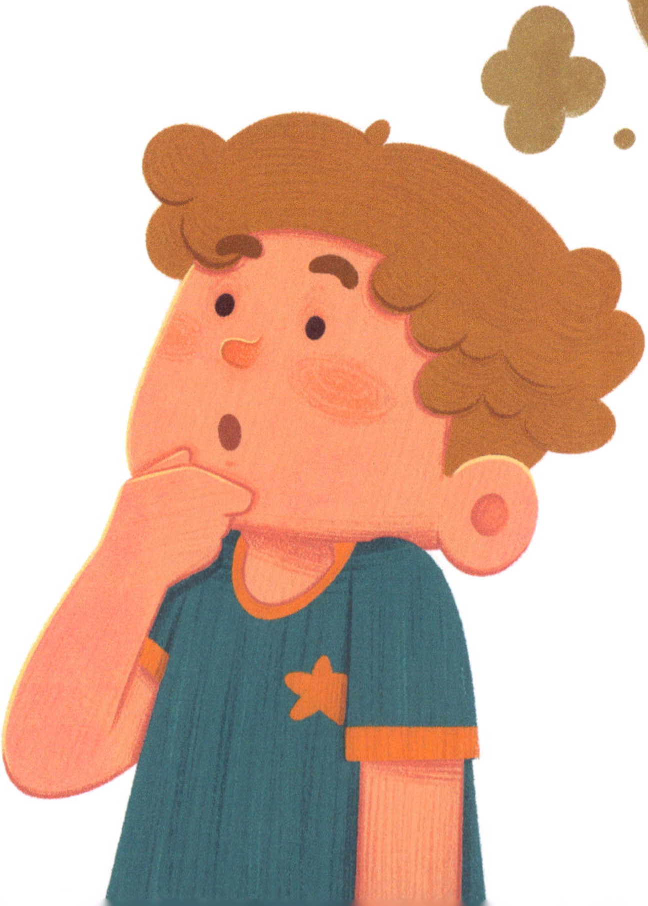

Let me tell you all about it.

In the very beginning, when God had just formed the earth, the sky, and the sea, He breathed life into dust from the ground, and it became a man—not just any man, but

ADAM,
the first man
God ever made.

The next thing that happened might come as a shock. You see, God took a rib from a sleeping Adam and used it to make

EVE,
the first woman of all creation!

I know this sounds suprising,

but it's absolutely true. Adam was made for important work. He was going to care for God's beautiful garden called Eden. Can you think of a better job?

Ever since then, God has been making boys.

Every boy you've ever known was made by God. From Adam to Abraham and all the way down to you, God has designed boys even while they grow in their mother's womb.

What is it exactly that gives a boy his boy-ness?

Is it the way he brushes his hair?
Or the clothes he wears?
No, it's nothing like that.

It's not even his strongest feelings. It's something that goes much deeper. It's woven into the tiniest inside parts of every boy.

Boys do have different bodies than girls. Yes, that's true. And the inside of a boy is different. You see, God's design can never be erased because it's written in his DNA.

When God makes a boy,

It's God's special design that says, "You are a boy."

But no two boys are exactly the same!

Some like to read or run really fast.
Some like to tell stories or sing on a stage.

And some boys like to dream up new ideas and take adventures *in God's big world.*

It can't be undone, this boy-ness of yours. It can't be hidden or even covered up. Your boy-ness goes with you wherever you are because you have that special design that says,

"I am a boy, and I was made by God."

It's a wonderful thing to be a boy like Adam,

tending to God's beautiful world just as He planned. And now that I've told you the truth about boys, I hope you see just how special you are.

When a baby boy is born and everyone smiles,

it's because they are so happy to see God's good plan right before their very eyes. And you, my son, are no exception. Your boy-ness shines bright from morning till night—

just as God intended.

About the Author

Kelsie Detweiler is a wife and thankful mom of two, who enjoys homeschooling her children, playing instruments, and spending time with her family and friends. She is passionate about discipling her children and hopes her writing will influence others to think biblically when it comes to cultural issues. When she's not doing these things, she is most likely drinking coffee, taking a walk, or scheming up new hobbies.

She can be found at www.kelsiedetweiler.com
and on Instagram @kelsiedetweiler.

Ambassador International's mission is to magnify the Lord Jesus Christ
and promote His Gospel through the written word.

We believe through the publication of Christian literature,
Jesus Christ and His Word will be exalted,
believers will be strengthened in their walk with Him,
and the lost will be directed to Jesus Christ as the only way of salvation.

For more information about
AMBASSADOR INTERNATIONAL
please visit:

www.ambassador-international.com
www.facebook.com/AmbassadorIntl
@AmbassadorIntl

Thank you for reading this book.
Please consider leaving us a review on your social media,
favorite retailer's website, Goodreads, Bookbub, or our website.

Also Available from Ambassador International

Theo is a chick condor, who wants to learn to fly like his mom and dad. But discouraging words from Raven cause him to doubt his ability. With each attempt, Theo loses sight of God's intention, only to succeed once he realizes, with the help of his parents, we can be who God made us to be!

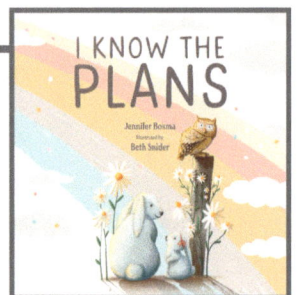

God has a plan for each child before they are even created. But in this noisy world, it's easy for our children to not hear God's voice and forget who they were created to be. *I Know the Plans* presents God's promises to young children with a fun, engaging rhyme, planting the seeds of Scripture into their hearts to help them grow in their love for Him. With vivid illustrations accompanying each passage, *I Know the Plans* captures a little one's attention from start to finish and should be the first book in every child's library.

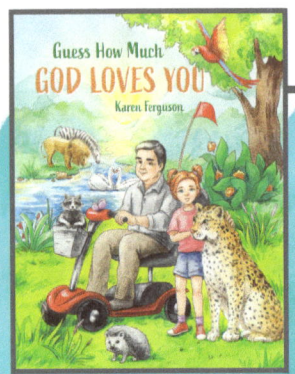

Guess How Much God Loves You is the story of seven-year-old Lucy Lu, a colorful, creatively curious first-grader, who is starting to have serious questions about God. How old is He? Does He sleep? What does He do all day? And the biggest one of all—does God love me? After one particularly hard day of being bullied by her classmates at school, Lucy feels like she doesn't matter. She sits with Papa Joe, who has promised to answer her questions about God, launching them onto a journey to discover God's never-changing, never-failing, never-ending love. What follows is a wild adventure through the Bible, where Lucy and her papa find themselves in the middle of each page of the exciting story of God's love and faithfulness for all people throughout all of history.

(continued endorsements)

"*God Made You, My Darling Boy* tenderly addresses gender identity in a way that even a child can understand. In this story, Detweiler lifts up the uniqueness of boyhood and its important place in our world. Readers are reminded that 'boy-ness' is a joy-filled gift given by the Creator to all of His male children. I personally recommend this book to anyone who wants to help their young son, nephew, or other special boy in their life to know God's love for him just the way he is!"

—Stephen Bradshaw, MBA, MA, Christian Ministry
Preaching Minister, Haigler St. Church of Christ
Abbeville, South Carolina

"In our confused culture, parents cannot wait to begin teaching their children the goodness of God's design for their bodies. This book is a great first step in building a biblical foundation on gender in the hearts of our sons."

—James Norris
Pastor, New Hope Presbyterian
Abbeville, South Carolina

"In *God Made You, My Darling Boy*, Kelsie beautifully communicates biblical truth. She accurately highlights that the men of the Bible were also created by God and that they had important work. This book is needed."

—Rachel Benham
Author and illustrator of *You Are Fearfully and Wonderfully Made*

"*God Made You, My Darling Boy* is an incredibly beautiful read for young boys! The message in this book shows just how special boys are, why God made them, and how vital they are in our lives. It is a sweet and heart-warming read to share with that special little boy in your life!"

—Yalixa Rodriguez
Author of *Mila & Mica Butterfly Cheese*

"A precious book celebrating God-given masculinity."

—Carmen Schober
Author

www.ingramcontent.com/pod-product-compliance
Lightning Source LLC
Chambersburg PA
CBHW061400090426
42743CB00002B/79